MORLA

CW01064970

COLOR BUTTERFLIES & MOTHS

A relaxing Coloring Book
To calm your mind and relieve stress

Follow us on
@morla.editions

First edition on July 2024

The total or partial reproduction of this work by any means or
procedure, including reprography and computer processing,
is expressly prohibited without the written authorization of the
copyright holders, under the sanctions established by law.

This book is made for your relaxation.

Let yourself go, feel free and enjoy.

Find out more titles to add to your collection:

COLOR BEAUTIFUL FLOWERS

A Relaxing Coloring Book

To calm your mind

and relieve stress

COLOR BEAUTIFUL BIRDS

A Relaxing Coloring Book

To calm your mind

and relieve stress

Scan the code with your phone to purchase them!

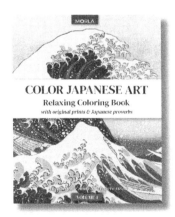

COLOR JAPANESE ART

Relaxing Coloring Book

with original prints

& Japanese proverbs

VOLUME 1

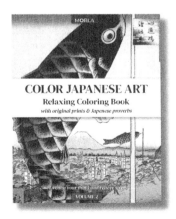

COLOR JAPANESE ART

Relaxing Coloring Book

with original prints

& Japanese proverbs

VOLUME 2

COLOR & LEARN from TOULOUSE-LAUTREC

Relaxing Coloring Book

with original prints

& quotes from the artist

MORLA

Morla Editions was created with the mission of bringing visual culture to the whole world.
We believe that creativity is the engine that drives innovation and originality. Every day, we passionately dedicate ourselves to exploring and expanding boundaries, understanding that the world around us is composed of images that speak, inspire, and educate.
Thus, each project we undertake is an opportunity to contribute to the vibrant visual dialogue that defines our era.

Follow us on
@morla.editions

If you enjoyed this coloring book, please consider leaving us a positive review on Amazon.
Your satisfaction is our goal, and your support means the world to us.

Thank you,
Morla Editions.

Printed in Great Britain
by Amazon